# Mervyn Wall

# THE IRISH WRITERS SERIES
## James F. Carens, General Editor

# MERVYN WALL

*Robert Hogan*

*Lewisburg*
**BUCKNELL UNIVERSITY PRESS**

Associated University Presses, Inc.
Cranbury, New Jersey 08512


Library of Congress Cataloging in Publication Data

Hogan, Robert Goode, 1930–
Mervyn Wall.

(The Irish writers series)
Bibliography:   p.
1.   Wall, Mervyn, 1908–
PR6045.A3255Z7         823′.9′12         72-175641
ISBN   0-8387-1065-4
ISBN   0-8387-1064-6   (pbk.)

Printed in the United States of America

# Contents

# Contents

# Preface

The Irish have a notoriously satiric bent, and, given
the conditions of their country at any time in the last
700 years, they have undoubtedly needed it. One finds
this satiric bent in their poems, their novels, their
plays, their newspapers, and their conversation. Sometimes the satire degenerates into sarcasm, or invective,
or mere vulgar abuse, but delightfully often it is
buoyed up by insight, wit, and a neat control of rhet-
oric. There is no dearth of satire in Irish writing, and
so when Vivian Mercier, for instance, calls Eimar
O'Duffy Ireland's only prose satirist, he is, I believe,
confusing manner with genre.

Satire is conventionally defined as a literary manner
which holds human follies and vices up to ridicule,
derision, or scorn. This is hardly a very adequate definition, for comedy itself is traditionally defined in
almost the same terms. As Goldoni put it, "Comedy
was invented to correct vices and to hold folly up to
ridicule. . . ." Obviously, satire and comedy are con-
fusingly and intricately related, and perhaps the most
convenient way of distinguishing between them is to

consider satire as a literary manner or technique, and comedy as a literary genre or form. Satire grows out of the attitude that the writer takes toward his material, while the arrangement and juxtaposition of the material itself constitutes the comic. This is far from a wholly satisfactory distinction, but it is a useful one.

Perhaps, though, one ought to go further and suggest that the genre of comedy contains satire, humor, parody, and wit as its chief manners. It is rather rare for a comic work to be almost wholly in one manner— as, for instance, Volpone seems to me almost wholly parodic, and *In Good King Charles' Golden Days* almost wholly witty. Most comedies, however, seem to contain significant proportions of two or more or all of the comic manners, and one might well wonder if the best comedies do not always have a pleasing balance of the various comic manners.

At any rate, there has been a good deal of confusion about satire because it has often been regarded as a literary form. Thus, traditionally, Jonathan Swift is a satiric writer, and *Gulliver's Travels* is a satire; while Richard Brinsley Sheridan is a comic writer, and *The Rivals* is a comedy. However, *The Rivals* contains a good deal of satire among its other comic elements of wit, parody, and humor. So it would probably be clearer not to speak of *Gulliver's Travels* as a satire and *The Rivals* as a comedy, but of *Gulliver's Travels* as a satiric fantasy and of *The Rivals* as a satiric comedy. When we make this dry, but not entirely academic distinction, we may begin to see why a writer like Mervyn Wall is a rare and valuable phenomenon in modern Irish literature.

In his novel *Leaves for the Burning,* Mervyn Wall
has written a serious realistic novel with many touches
of satire; in his novel *No Trophies Raise,* he has written a satiric comedy with some touches of wit, humor,
and effectively uncomic sentiment; in *The Unfortunate
Fursey* and *The Return of Fursey,* however, he has
wedded the manner of satire to the genre of fantasy
rather than of comedy. This wedding makes him both
interesting and memorable.

Fantasy, I take it, is a literary work usually, but not
necessarily, dramatic or fictional in form, and contain-
ing in whole or in part a suspension of the ordinary
laws of reality. If a serious play or novel depends upon
the author's vision of what reality is like, and if a
comic play or novel depends upon the author's vision
of what reality should be like, then a fantastic play or
novel depends upon an author's vision of what it would
be interesting for reality to be like. Many fantasies
create entirely new worlds of their own, such as Alice's
Wonderland, in which the ordinary laws governing the
universe and society are superseded by others of the
author's whimsical invention. A fantasy often is whimsical, frivolous, and merely entertaining, but it can
also be dour, grim, and quite pertinent. Like any ordinary tale, it may even contain within itself a gamut of
tones, ranging from the silly to the caustic, from the
airy to the sordid, from the farcical to the tragic. Not
all of the fantasies in Irish literature are satiric. Seumas
O'Kelly's stories in *The Leprechaun of Kilmeen* have
an attitude of merry *laissez-faire,* rather than of criticism about them. Spike Milligan's novel *Puckoon*—
which, I suppose, must be considered an Irish novel, is

basically a nonsensical jape. A good many of Lord Dunsany's fantasies seem designed to evoke wonder or a kind of lyrical beauty.

Fantasy is not, of course, everybody's cup of tea. The form is so arbitrary and so individual that it alienates many readers who are uncomfortable without the familiar feel of reality in their fiction. To the literal-minded, fantasy, because it could not happen, is therefore not worth contemplation. Satire has never been universally popular either. For one thing, its statement is often implicit rather than overt, and it uncomfortably pushes one to serious grapplings with morality. When the manner of satire, then, is wedded to the form of fantasy, the result is not inevitably a popular success, and that fact may partially explain the relative obscurity of Mervyn Wall.

Although there is an immense amount of the satiric in modern Irish writing, there is relatively little satiric fantasy apart from that great touchstone, *Gulliver's Travels*. What there is, however, is extraordinarily distinguished. A list would have to include James Stephens's much-loved *The Crock of Gold,* a bit of Dunsany, some of the best plays of George Fitzmaurice, the best play of John Synge, Eimar O'Duffy's brilliant Cuandine trilogy, and Joyce's amazing masterpiece *Finnegans Wake.* In recent years, the work of two neo-Joyceans has come into its own. Samuel Beckett's much admired prose fictions and plays would seem appropriate to include here because his inimitable world is a dourly fantastic gloss on our own, and because his attitude, if not always satiric, is most assuredly wry. Brian

O'Nolan, under the pseudonym of Myles na gCopaleen, wrote a delicious newspaper column called *Cruiskeen Lawn* which must be listed here, just as surely as the four superb novels he wrote under his other pseudonym of Flann O'Brien. There are also the last plays and long portions of the last autobiographies of Sean O'Casey; there are Denis Johnston's remarkable plays *The Old Lady Says "No!"*, *Bride for the Unicorn*, and even *The Golden Cuckoo;* there is Donagh Mac-Donagh's *Happy as Larry,* as well as some of Padraic Fallon's radio plays and one of John O'Donovan's political satires; and surely it would not overly stretch our term to include the world of Brendan Behan's *The Hostage.*

These names at least should be mentioned, and if this is not a lengthy list it is an inordinately distinguished one. The point of the following pages is that one of the most honorable names on it must be that of Mervyn Wall.

# Acknowledgments

Grateful acknowledgment is made to Methuen & Co., Ltd., for permission to quote from *Leaves for the Burning* and *No Trophies Raise*. My thanks also to the University of Delaware for a summer fellowship to work on this book, to my friends John and Vera O'Donovan, and, of course, to Mr. and Mrs. Mervyn Wall for much kindness, patience and hospitality.

R. H.

# Chronology

| | |
|---|---|
| 1908 | Born August 23 in Dublin. |
| 1916 | Enters Belvedere College. |
| 1922–1924 | Studies in Bonn. |
| 1925–1928 | Enters University College, Dublin, graduates with a B.A. |
| 1934 | Enters Irish Civil Service. |
| 1937 | *Alarm among the Clerks* produced by the Abbey Theatre's Experimental Theatre at the Peacock. |
| 1941 | *The Lady in the Twilight* produced at the Abbey Theatre. |
| 1945 | *The Shadow* produced by the Players Theatre in the Olympia Theatre, Dublin. |
| 1946 | *The Unfortunate Fursey* published. |
| 1948 | Wall joins Radio Eireann; *The Return of Fursey* published. |
| 1950 | Marries Fanny Feehan. |
| 1952 | *Leaves for the Burning* published. |
| 1956 | *No Trophies Raise* published. |
| 1957 | Transfers to the Arts Council. |

# Chronology

# Mervyn Wall

# *I*

Mervyn Wall was born on August 23, 1908, in Dublin. His father was a barrister who, having independent means, did not practice. Although the Wall home was Roman Catholic, it was also urban and middleclass, and so young Wall had little early exposure to the literary and nationalist ferment of those fervent years. Irish legends and myths and the whole background of the Gaelic, peasant Ireland were alien to him, and much that he learned of his own country, he learned in later years from observing productions at the Abbey Theatre.

When Wall was eight years old, he was entered in Belvedere College, the Jesuit school so faithfully portrayed in James Joyce's *Portrait of the Artist as a Young Man* and in Conal O'Riordan's *Adam of Dublin*. At fourteen he was sent to Germany, where he stayed for two years, from 1922 to 1924, with a family in Bonn. He was not enrolled in a school, and so never really came to grips with some of the more usual academic subjects. He did learn German, however, and he did read avidly. Although this was still the time of the

French occupation and the country was still impoverished from the war, it was a time for Wall himself of romantic adventure. It was a considerable disappointment, then, to be brought back to Dublin for a final year at Belvedere, and after so much freedom to decline again into being a schoolboy.

After Belvedere, Wall did medicine for a year at University College, Dublin, but found the study uncongenial and worked instead for a B.A., which he received in 1928. In college, his particular friends were the young poets Denis Devlin and Brian Coffey. Devlin especially influenced him by introducing him to the poems of Pound and Eliot. Nevertheless, Wall's original literary bent was for the drama. He was head of the university dramatic society, and Synge, whose Wicklow mountains he had often tramped over, was his great enthusiasm. As with many young men, this was a time of reading, of discovery, and of an excitement never to be quite recaptured again.

Upon graduation, he had no profession, for a B.A. then, as now, opened few doors. These were the depression years, and people took what jobs they could get. Wall was helped by his father, who had become extremely religious and involved in many charitable organizations in his middle years. The elder Wall belonged to a secret organization of Catholic laymen called the Knights of Columbanus. This was a kind of religious Ku Klux Klan, and its jobbery Wall was later to score fiercely in his novel *No Trophies Raise*. At any rate, with the backing of this group, he secured a clerkship in the Agricultural Credit Corporation, where he worked from 1930 to 1932.

In 1934, he entered the Irish Civil Service, and there he stayed for fourteen years, until he was thirty-nine. Undoubtedly, all civil services are dreary and monotonous, but in Ireland, where the writers, artists and actors could rarely live off the income from their art, the Civil Service position was often a necessary livelihood. George Fitzmaurice, for instance, was a Civil Servant for most of his days. Other Irish writers, such as T. C. Murray, Paul Vincent Carroll, Bryan Mac-Mahon, Brian Friel and Tom Coffey have been teachers. Many others, particularly in the 1940s and 1950s, were connected, as was Wall, with Radio Eireann or with one of the Dublin newspapers. In more recent years, many writers have in some fashion or other been connected with Telefís Eireann. Of all the forms of work allied to writing, however, a Civil Service clerkship must surely be among the more uncongenial. These years of stultifying routine, of dealings with boorish and uneducated officials, of martinetish protocol quite as rigorous as that of any army, left a mark upon Wall and upon practically all of his work. His best-known play, *Alarm among the Clerks,* is directly about this life in an office; the middle-aged hero of his novel *Leaves for the Burning* is a low-grade County Council employee, the old philosopher in *No Trophies Raise* is a pathetic victim of the Civil Service; and even in the two Fursey fantasies there is some passing satire about the medieval equivalent of the Civil Service.

In three years of clerking in Dublin Castle, Wall did manage to write a handful of short stories which were published in American and English magazines, such as *Harper's, Collier's* and *Argosy.* Such occasional income was a godsend to an underpaid Civil Servant, whose salary was originally only £130 a year, and who by 1946 had risen to only £350 a year. His first story, incidentally, "They Also Serve," is set in Dublin Castle, and is a charming satire of Civil Service bureaucracy.

In 1937, Wall's play *Alarm among the Clerks* was staged by the Abbey Theatre's experimental wing in the Peacock, for a short run of a week. It was a critical success, but, nevertheless, the Abbey Experimental Theatre immediately afterwards became dormant for four years. On May 19, his play *The Lady in the Twilight* was played at the Abbey for a short run of one week.

In 1946, Wall's playful first novel, *The Unfortunate Fursey,* appeared. Shortly afterwards, he was transferred to Sligo. Sean O'Faolain thought this was in retribution for Wall's writing, but in fact it was probably brought about quite innocently from the attempt of the novelist Peadar O'Donnell to secure a transfer for a friend. Wall, being unmarried, was easily transferrable. At any rate, this exile to the provinces was enormously disheartening to a Dublinman used to the conviviality and the conversation of the capital. For a few months, Wall was returned to Dublin, but then transferred back to Sligo and then to an obscure post in Manorhamilton.

Wall's feelings about his provincial surroundings were to be dourly reflected in much of the novel *Leaves for the Burning*.

In 1948, Francis MacManus the novelist and Robert Farren the poet helped to arrange Wall's transfer to Radio Eireann in Dublin, of which they were both officials. Wall became MacManus's assistant in the General Features department, planning programs and recording them. He stayed at this post for nine years, churning out a succession of talks and documentaries. Although the standards for these programs were perhaps not of the highest, Wall describes these years as pleasant ones. He was able to meet most of the literary men in the country, for practically all of them at one time or another would be connected with the radio. There he also met his future wife, Fanny Feehan, a musician and music critic, whom he married in 1950 and who has borne him four children. But although the work was congenial, it was also demanding, and the salary was quite low. To supplement it, Wall turned to writing talks, book reviews and documentaries, and to broadcasting many of them himself. One series of seventy-two broadcasts was called *Along Many a Mile,* and was composed of chatty, historical talks about the Irish countryside. Also, sometime in the 1950s, Radio Eireann produced his play *Wicklow Granite.*

In 1957, when Sean O'Faolain was appointed to the Arts Council, he secured Wall's appointment there as secretary, or chief executive, a post which he still holds.

In addition to his four novels, his plays, and his

short stories, Wall has done a large amount of journal-
ism and reviewing in Irish periodicals, such as *The
Irish Times, The Irish Press, Hibernia, Irish Writing,*
and *The Bell.* Currently he writes a radio column for
*The Irish Press.* As Secretary of Yeats' Academy of
Letters, he has breathed some new life into that rather
dormant organization by securing it a regular income
and by arranging for the award of an annual prize of
£250 to a promising young writer.

# II

Wall's first published work was a short story, "They Also Serve," which was published in *Harper's* in 1940. Since then, over the years he has published in various Irish, American and English periodicals eight other short stories and also one extract from an abandoned novel. The stories are about his usual topics and preoccupations. They offer wry or glum glimpses of the Civil Service, or they ponder the drab life of the middle-aged, or sometimes they are mild comic fantasies about the vaguely supernatural. The best of them are probably "They Also Serve," "The Hogskin Gloves," "Cloonaturk," "Leo the Terror" and "The Demon Angler." All of them are engaging, neatly turned and smoothly written. They seem to accomplish exactly what the author wanted, and if collected they would make a pleasing little book. There are no strong effects or deep probings in them, and there are no masterpieces. On the other hand, O'Flaherty, O'Connor and O'Faolain have all published some stories that are not so good as some of these.

Wall's real debut as a writer, however, came with the

production of his play *Alarm among the Clerks,* which
was first performed in the Peacock Theatre on April 5,
1937, by the Abbey's Experimental Theatre. *The Irish
Independent* called it "unlike anything else in Irish
drama," and Austin Clarke in a short Foreword to the
printed text placed Wall in "that group of younger
Irish dramatists who are in revolt against the stock
country themes of Abbey drama." The point was well
taken, for apart from its quite solid merits as theatre,
the play will certainly always warrant an affirmative
paragraph in the histories of the modern Irish drama
because of its unique subject. This was really the first
Irish drama to treat the grey monotony and quiet de-
spair that fill the life of the modern urban office worker.
This was a milieu far removed from the peasant cot-
tages that Synge, Colum and Lady Gregory had written
about in the early days of the dramatic movement, and
it was equally far removed from O'Casey's mouldering
tenements in Mountjoy Square.

The play's longest and best act is the first, which is
set in an office of a Dublin bank. This act shows us
with convincing verisimilitude the first hour or so in a
perfectly routine day. The dialogue is simple, even
flat, as indeed it would need to be for such necessary
interchanges as the following:

> FOX: Some help is required in the public office. The Di-
> rector has just rung Mr. Ireton. Now, let me see.
> You're on the return, Mr. Selskar?
> SELSKAR: Yes.
> FOX: Well, the rest of you better go across to the public
> office now, and, when the job is done, come back here at

once. No delaying. There's plenty to be done here. *Exeunt* MULLEN *and* DOODY *R. Exit* FINN *back with letters.*

FOX: Miss Boyd is over with the Director. Mr. Selskar, when Miss Noone comes back, tell her to go across to the public office too. Are you nearly finished that return yourself?

At first glance, such an account about something inordinately boring in itself would seem doomed to be boring to readers or to viewers. When Elmer Rice handled precisely the same kind of material in *The Adding Machine,* he devoted only one scene to it rather than, as Wall does, nearly half of his play. Also, Rice used such devices as the interior monologue for its irony, and a comic heightening of emotion for its satire. In other words, Rice avoided the danger of tedium by heightening the essentials of the scene for its comic-caustic effect.

Wall, on the other hand, limited himself in his first act entirely to the tools of the realist, and so, although his effects are not so spectacularly dramatic, they have a strong cumulative persuasiveness. He quite successfully avoids dullness by a number of small strategies. A good deal of the sporadic conversation that goes on in an office is actually not about the work at hand, but about a multitude of other topics. Wall cannily uses such chunks of conversation to illuminate his characters as well as to contrast the cold and formal inhumanity of office routine with the very different actuality that lies so near the surface. One character's bad jokes, another's tardiness, another's petty irritation about losing his pen are all details which both characterize and at the same time imply that something is quite drastically wrong with this milieu.

Wall also keeps his characterization, exposition, and illustration of monotony from being static or dull by a basic thread of conflict to which nearly every situation and every character in the scene is attached. Each of the clerks and typists is under a constant pressure from above. There is a constant threat to the dignity of each, if not indeed to their livelihood. This pressure for a constant driving efficiency is enforced by the chief clerk, Mr. Fox, and by the department manager, Mr. Ireton, who periodically erupts into the room from his own office and makes some irascible demand. Later in the play we learn that Fox is actually delighted with his staff and thinks it the most efficient he ever had. This fact is quite thoroughly camouflaged, however, for the technique of Fox and Ireton is to indicate constant dissatisfaction with the office work, so that all of the clerks live under an ever-present threat of dismissal. This browbeating is no personal vendetta, but simply the means by which Fox and Ireton seek to maintain efficiency. Wall's point, of course, is that such an atmosphere is intolerable and degrading.

He makes this point implicitly by the illustrative action of the first act, and overtly by the pub conversation of the clerks in the second act. With the exception of one quiescent, beaten-down old man, we see that each of the clerks in the second act has chosen some sort of defense against the impersonal system. However, we see each of these defenses through the eyes of Selskar, the clerk who had been late for work in the first act and who is the closest to being broken by the system. Through Selskar's eyes, we see that each of these defenses is inadequate.

When the other clerks return to work, Selskar, who is now drunk, remains behind; and the entirety of the third act takes place in his mind. In the third-act daydream, Selskar returns to the office and, like Zero in Rice's *Adding Machine,* kills the boss. In actuality, however, nothing has happened except that it is now certain that Selskar has lost his job; and Wall's point about the intolerable but inexorable triumph of the system is very painfully made.

The dream or the fantasy which escapes from reality or triumphs over reality is very central to Wall's writing. Both of his Fursey books are essentially such escapist fantasies, and to hazard a generalization it is certainly possible that the circumstances of Wall's own life, which for long periods he undoubtedly regarded as both intolerable and inescapable, determined his strategy for dealing with reality at the remove of the satiric fantasy.

*Alarm among the Clerks,* save for the melodrama of the conclusion, is a low-keyed play, but one which clings persistently in the memory.

Wall's *The Lady in the Twilight* was first produced at the Abbey Theatre on May 19, 1941. It was directed by Frank Dermody, and had Fred Johnson, Harry Brogan, Ria Mooney, Joan Plunkett, Denis O'Dea, Michael J. Dolan, F. J. McCormick, Liam Redmond and Gerard Healy in the cast.

The play is set in the 1930s in West Wicklow. Its title refers to some lost ideal that has eluded each of the main characters. The production was not particularly successful, but Denis Johnston in a review in *The Bell* admired its Chekhovian subtley. The play does not seem to me especially Chekhovian in technique, although its quiet somberness of tone, and its general aura of passive resignation is superficially Chekhovian.

The play's action is rather minimal, and indeed Wall does not so much create a story as set up a situation which reveals character. There is, however, one startling incident to which the characters revealingly react.

Malachy Ross is a vain and impoverished pseudo-writer of a type not unusual in Ireland. He writes little or nothing and lives with his second wife, an ex-dancer, and his frail daughter in a cottage in West Wicklow. There is considerable agitation among the local farmers to have the Land Commission break up the big estate of Glengesh House, and distribute it among the small farmers. Edward Allen, a writer and idealistic agitator, arrives with his son to hold a meeting supporting the farmers, but they, inflamed by an eccentric and reactionary old parish priest, disrupt his meeting. Much of this action takes place offstage, however, and the first act is largely given over to introducing the characters and to exposition. Indeed, practically all of the second act is also given over to a deeper probing of character. The second act takes place in the Big House, a few rooms of which are still kept open by Phillip Vane, an amiable and cultivated futility of a man, who is acting as caretaker. The act ends with the most notable action of the play. Vane has just sung a moving and poignant ballad, and the others are sitting quiet and touched by it. Just as they are about to clap, a shot comes through the window, and he falls dead.

In the third act, the murderer, a young farmer, asks Allen for help to escape to Dublin. Refused, he leaves, attempting to cross the mountains on foot, but as they are covered with great drifts of snow he inevitably leaves to his death.

The point of the act and of the play is that the ideals of the Church as exemplified by the old priest, of art as exemplified by Malachy Ross, and of social justice as exemplified by Edward Allen, were each ineffectual and misleading in their effect on the young farmer. Each failed him, and, as the exemplar of pure practicality, Egan the detective, points out, the action of the murder was itself quite pointless. In another year or eighteen months, the Government would quietly distribute the land. This ineffectuality of the ideal is paralleled by the plight of Ross's young daughter Verna, who has fallen in love with Allen's son Raymond. However, Raymond plans to escape from his father's carefully laid plans for his life to be socially useful, by running away for five years to South America. He asks Verna to wait, but she realizes with a sad stoicism that in five years she will probably be dead.

The general effect of the play is one of pervasive defeatism. It is a sadly pessimistic view of life such as people say one finds in Chekhov, but it is unleavened by Chekhov's masterly sardonic comedy, by his genial eye for the ridiculous, by his brilliantly ironic juxtapositions of incongruities. Chekhov's perhaps similar view in *The Cherry Orchard* or *The Three Sisters* is conveyed by disparate tones of farce, comedy, melodrama, and even tragedy. His pessimism has a detachment rising out of the disparities which his comic and realistic eye detected in life. Wall's play, on the other hand, sees little of this variety, and allows an almost purely pessimistic conclusion to permeate all of the incidents of the play. I am not, of course, adopting the stance that Wall should have regarded life differently; I am simply pointing out that because of his attitude his play is written in much the same tone throughout. He does perceive incongruities that do not jibe with the prevailing tone of the play, but his perception here is much more muted than is Chekhov's, and so his play is, I think, less rich in texture.

The strength of the play lies in its characterization, rather than in its plot or in its not particularly notable dialogue. Most of the characters are better and more fully drawn than one expects in a play, but Wall's undoubted triumph is the character of Malachy Ross. It would have been an admirable feat of broad stage satire merely to have put an Irish poetaster on the boards, with all of his arrogance, petty vanity, pettish temper, and fantastic fluency which in this instance is padded out with unacknowledged borrowings from the mots of real writers. It would have been admirable merely to have juxtaposed these qualities against a nearly total lack of accomplishment. This in itself would have made a salutary and telling satire of the Irish man about letters, but Wall has with Ross done a good deal more.

By refusing to let Ross remain merely as a clever-stupid man, he has left the hard Molière-Jonson realm of brilliant stage caricature, and moved into the high realm of stage art, the realm of Ibsen and Chekhov. Ross, with all of his faults, is clever, is perceptive, has some passion, had at one time a real vision of the ideal, and even now, when he is full of sentimental self-dramatization, the self-pity arises from things that he realizes were valuable to lose. Ross is a superb character, and one of the most fully drawn in recent Irish drama. Denis Johnston himself would, I think, have been happy to have created this character.

The play taken as a whole is not a great play, but it is good enough to demand comparison with the best—with, say, Johnston's *The Moon in the Yellow River*. *The Lady in the Twilight* lacks a really engrossing plot. It lacks polish of dialogue. It lacks wit. It lacks diversity of tone. And the uncompromising greyness of its view might well make it a dismal experience for the conventional audience. Nevertheless, it is a very good play, with an excellently startling second act curtain (rather, in fact, like the second act curtain of *The Moon in the Yellow River*) , a movingly muted final curtain, and a triumph of characterization in Malachy Ross.

*The Shadow* was produced by the Players Theatre, an interesting but short-lived group, in the Olympia Theatre, Dublin, in 1945. The author's only copy of the script has gone astray, and so perhaps little more can be said other than that the play was received respectfully but not enthusiastically, in what *The New York Times* would call today "mixed notices." For instance, A. J.

Leventhal, writing in *The Dublin Magazine,* admired the craftsmanship and the characterization, but also said:

> . . . the whole production, like damp fireworks, failed to light up. Perhaps it was that there was no real warmth in the dramatist himself. Caught up in the external design of his play in its geometric symbols, he was like some aphasic magician unable to produce the ultimate abracadabra to raise the spirit of genuine drama. It was not the association of the plot with the life and death of a local politician of recent times that put the audience into ill-humour but the fact that there was no real life, no real politics, no real love, even no real humour. . . .

The local politician of recent times, whom Leventhal refers to, was Kevin O'Higgins.

*Wicklow Granite,* Wall's last play, is an historical piece laid mainly in 1798, during Wolfe Tone's rebellion. It concerns the rebel leader Joseph Holt, who fought a guerilla warfare in the Wicklow mountains, and it is a straightforward piece with a more developed and conventional action than either *Alarm among the Clerks* or *The Lady in the Twilight.* But, although the play has a sufficient abundance of properly placed incidents, its great weakness lies in the enormous length of many of its speeches. The style of the dialogue is perfectly adequate, if in no place notably individual or brilliant, but the astonishing length of many speeches poses an extremely difficult problem for a director.

The excellence of this play is also its characterization. Unlike *The Lady in the Twilight,* however, which had no one main character, *Wicklow Granite* stands solidly and solely on the character of Holt, who is drawn with such a convincing diversity of contradictory impulses that he nearly succeeds in making the play really memorable.

Holt is a self-righteous Presbyterian, full of self-esteem and occasionally sincere feelings about religion. He is, however, incongruously forced to join the United Irishmen when the yeomanry burn his house. He is a pillar of society forced out of his proper niche. He is a patriot in spite of himself. He is also a man of much force and vitality. Quickly he becomes the leader of the rebels in the Wicklow mountains. The contradiction in his character is that he is not basically a nationalist but a royalist. He is perfectly consistent by his own lights, refusing when he surrenders to denounce Michael Dwyer or his other colleagues whom he thought sincere, but denouncing those whom he considered mere marauders and robbers. Holt is, although he is never able to understand the fact, only a half-patriot. With proper justice, he is not condemned to death as was Tone, but merely transported for a number of years. Yet although he betrayed the cause of which he was a leader, he cannot understand why the Irish do not consider him a hero.

Holt also has a mass of interesting minor contradictions. He is a pious family man who is also something of a lecher. He is grandly self-sacrificing and pettily vain. He is bloodthirsty and merciful. In sum, he is a remarkably well-drawn character, and the play is primarily an extended delineation of him. In that attempt, Wall is perfectly successful, but character drawing without any more broadly meaningful point is probably not enough.

# III

Wall's first novel, *The Unfortunate Fursey,* is a sprightly, sunny, ingenious, good-hearted satire, which will probably remain for most readers Wall's most appealing book. Its hero, Fursey, is a rotund, white-haired, unprepossessing medieval lay-brother in the monastery of Clonmacnoise. He is regarded as so negligible by his community that he is relegated to the simplest task in the kitchen, paring edible roots, "and even at that, it could not be truthfully claimed that he excelled." Fursey's medieval world is populated not only by difficult, irascible, and violent people, but also by sorcerers, witches, demons, devils, and vampires. Most of these characters, both natural and supernatural, manage to be both engaging and malevolent, and yet in a general sense this fey and broadly drawn world is not at all unlike our own.

Fursey himself is an unassuming fellow of no particular abilities—not strong, not handsome, not witty, not wise—who in his simple, amiable way only desires to continue harmlessly and helpfully through life. Unhappily for him, as for many of us, the world does not always allow such an ostrich-like life. Fursey is uprooted and made to scramble for a perilous existence in a world he never made and against powers that are undependable, intractable, and malignant. The forces upon which it would seem he could most rely for protection, the Church and the State, actually combine to throw him into the hands of witches, sorcerers, and devils, and then proceed to persecute him for having joined the powers of darkness. The character most amiably disposed toward Fursey is not his abbot or his king, but the devil himself. However, after a series of fantastic misfortunes, Fursey emerges from this unequal and unwished-for contest as improbably and magnificently triumphant.

The quality of the book depends, of course, upon the ingenuity of its invention, and Wall's imagination is delightfully fertile in conjuring up whimsical and slyly satiric details. Briefly, the details of the story are these: the devil decides to launch an all-out assault upon the holy monastery of Clonmacnoise. Consequently, the good monks are assailed by "imps and ghouls, night fiends, goblins and all sorts of hellish phantoms. . . ."

> For fifteen successive days Clonmacnoise was haunted horribly. It became commonplace for a monk on turning a corner to be confronted by a demon who saluted him with cuffs and blows. Hydras, scorpions, ounces and pards frequented the cells, and serpents filled the passages with their hissings and angry sibilations. The nights were hideous with a horrid hubbub, a clattering of wrenching doors, and the howls and shrieks of invisible beings.

Being repulsed by the monks, the devil decides to make a breach in the wall of sanctity by concentrating on its weakest point, Fursey. Fursey unfortunately has a slight speech impediment which prevents him from instantly dispelling the devil's forces by prayer. Indeed, the effect of the gryphon who enters his cell, the various four- and six-legged creatures, the incubus who seats itself "without much apparent enthusiasm" on his chest, the various undraped females, and the black gentleman with the slight limp is to drive him nearly out of his wits and render him quite speechless anyway.

> Brother Fursey's brain simmered in his head as he tried to remember the form of adjuration, but the only words that he could bring to mind were those of the abbot's injunction: "Be not over-confident in yourself and presumptuously daring."

The abbot and the other monks decide that the most efficacious way of ridding the monastery of the devil and his various fiends is to rid themselves of Fursey, and so he is set loose in a world for which he is most ill-equipped. His first adventure is to rescue the Gray Mare, an ancient and repulsive witch, whom the Church and the State are dunking in a pond. When the authorities become convinced, quite erroneously, that the Gray Mare is harmless, they decide to dispose of the difficult problem of Fursey by marrying him to her. Fortunately for Fursey, his nuptial bliss is interrupted by a feud which his wife has with Cuthbert, a neighboring sorcerer who innocently passes as the village sexton. After various horrendous supernatural alarums and excursions, the Gray Mare expires, giving Fursey a parting kiss which transfers her powers to him.

Sorcery, of course, is a profession which requires diligent study and application, and so the only immediate effect of Fursey's transformation is his inheritance of Albert, his wife's familiar, an ungainly, shaggy, doglike beast with bear paws. Albert, Fursey soon discovers, is an acquisition of dubious merit, since he requires, in order to render efficient service, a frequent feeding of blood from a supernumerary nipple Fursey has now acquired. By his own lights, Albert is a basically amiable creature and regards Fursey's horror of witchcraft as foolish and perverse.

> Albert shambled over to the edge of the bed. Fursey put out his hand and patted him on the head. Albert wagged his hindquarters delightedly, and his smoky red eyes lit up with expectancy.
> "Breakfast?" he repeated hopefully.
> "No," reiterated Fursey.
> Albert looked aggrieved. "If you expect nimble and courteous service from me," he asserted plaintively, "you'll have to keep me fed. I'm that thirsty, the tongue is fair hanging out of my mouth for a drop of blood."
> "That's enough of that," rejoined Fursey.

Fursey's abilities as a sorcerer include only two rudimentary powers. He is able to produce any kind or quantity of food or drink by tossing a rope over a tree branch or convenient beam, and he learns, at considerable personal peril, how to ride a broomstick. At the first opportunity, he mounts his broomstick, escapes from the tutelage of Cuthbert, and flies back to Clonmacnoise to throw himself on the mercy of his mentor, the abbot. However, the abbot knows that there is only one thing to do with a confessed sorcerer, and that is to turn him over to the proper authorities for trial and inevitable burning.

When, however, Fursey attempts to plead guilty, the prosecutor, Father Furiosus, refuses to accept the plea because, "Witnesses have come here at great trouble and expense, and they can't be sent home again after a trial lasting only six minutes. Anyway, the accused is entitled to a fair trial." Still, Furiosus does concede that, "If the accused should be found not guilty after the evidence has been considered . . . we will start again at the beginning and accept his plea of guilty."

After various ghastly dunkings, beatings, and roastings, Fursey manages with the help of his only ally, the devil, to escape. He finds himself a job as farmboy and promptly falls in love with Maeve, the daughter of the house. When he learns that she is shortly to be married to a swaggering, handsome brute named Magnus, he leaves disconsolately for Cashel to give himself up.

On the way there, he encounters a saintly hermit and a grisly monster, and it is debatable which is the more appalling. The hermit, named the Gentle Anchorite, has an odor of sanctity that is almost overpowering in any confined space, and his idea of a feast is an uncrackable bread crust and a mouldy hazel nut (and he regards the mouldy part as the more toothsome). The monster is an irascible green creature with homicidal tendencies named Joe the Poltergeist. Escaping from both perils, Fursey arrives at Cashel where the devil is concluding a sort of nonaggression pact with the Irish clergy. Despite these tolerant overtures towards evil, the clergy are still, to Fursey's surprise, determined to burn him as a sorcerer, and so he becomes uncharacteristically angry. He escapes on a broomstick after igniting the roof of the bishop's palace, and flies off to rescue Maeve at the altar. Quickly dispatching Magnus with a couple of deft kicks, Fursey tosses Maeve across his broomstick and heads for Britain:

> Then he flew eastwards, over the grey-green fields, the crooked roads and the sluggishly rolling mountains of Ireland, the first of many exiles for whom a decent way of living was not to be had in their own country.

Such a summary of the bones of the plot can do little but indicate a certain basically fey imagination. The strength of the book, however, lies even more in its individual details. Here, Wall is consistently admirable, and the volume is filled with a multitude of touches which are either appealingly fantastic or drolly satiric. I know of no really sound way to indicate how richly textured the novel is, and must fall back upon two typical illustrations. There is a short and casual paragraph in Chapter IX in which, quite in passing, Wall makes a neat satiric thrust at a familiar Dublin phenomenon.

> Fursey listened to the conversation which came up to them from the far end of the tavern. A small man who was the centre of an admiring group, was holding up to ridicule all writers alive and dead, punctuating his witticisms and sallies with bursts of cackling laughter which made Fursey shudder. As Fursey glanced in his direction, he recognized with alarm the gargoyle whom he had seen in Cuthbert's garden. . . .

"Oh, you know him," remarked the anchorite apparently relieved. "I feared from his appearance that he was a petty demon of the trickier sort."

"I know him slightly," responded Fursey nervously. "He's a minor man of letters."

Although the novel is rich in such deft touches of satire, its highly individual quality, its great warmth and geniality, arises primarily from the whimsy, the totally unsatiric flights of imagination purely for its own sake. This quality I should like to illustrate by a rather more extensive quote, Cuthbert's recipe for escaping from a basilisk:

"When I was quite a young man," began Cuthbert, "I was out walking one evening along a country road, when on turning a corner I came suddenly on a basilisk rambling along by himself enjoying, I suppose, the mild evening air. Fortunately I recognised him at once for what he was, and knowing that the gaze of a basilisk turns one to stone if one is so foolish as to meet it, I immediately dropped my eyes and fixed them on a spot on the road midway between his front two hooves. At the same time I bent rapidly and picked up from the ground a piece of straight stick which was lying to hand."

"And did you feel no ill-effect from his gaze?" asked Fursey breathlessly.

"I felt a certain chill," conceded Cuthbert, "and I cannot say but that an occasional twinge of rheumatism which I get to the present day is not the result of his survey. However, my whole being told me that I must act with the utmost despatch; so, holding the piece of stick vertically at arm's length, I advanced it rapidly to the tip of his nose. I did not dare look up, but I judged accurately where the tip of his nose must be, by keeping my eyes directed on a spot on the road midway between his front hooves. As you know, the instinct of both animal and human is to keep the eyes fixed on any object that is rapidly approaching. A basilisk's eyes are protuberant, so that by the time the vertical stick had reached his nose, his two protuberant eyes were looking inward at one another, and he effectively turned himself into stone. When I ventured to look up, there was a very fine specimen of a young bull basilisk in stone with his eyes crossed."

"Dear me," ejaculated Fursey.

"He remained there for many years, much admired by the besotted peasantry, and an object of great interest to visitors. Finally he was discovered by an archaeologist who had lost his way one 'night. A learned paper was written, and a whole school of archaeologists descended on the neighbourhood from the monastery of Cong. They took measurements and drew pictures of him, and wrote several shelves of learned volumes. I understand that they argued his presence proved the early inhabitants of this island to have come from the land of Egypt, where such monuments abound. The fact that his eyes were looking into one another interested them greatly; and they deduced from that fact that the religion of our Egyptian forefathers laid great stress on the virtues of introspection."

"Is he there still?" asked Fursey.

"Unfortunately," replied Cuthbert, "some years later the local authorities broke him up for road metal. As you are no doubt aware, material considerations in this country always outweigh considerations of antiquarian interest. I thought it was a pity myself. He was an interesting and unusual monument of our past and was of considerable importance to the local tourist industry."

"Well," averred Fursey, "I'll know what to do if I ever meet a basilisk."

The satire of the book is quite as broad and cartoon-like as that of O'Duffy in the Cuandine trilogy, but Wall's target is smaller. His medieval Ireland is, of course, a gloss upon the Ireland of his own time, and his diagnosis of Ireland's ills seems to find the Irish clergy at the

root of most of them. Criticisms of the clergy permeate
the book, but they are most devastatingly phrased in
the pact between the clergy and the devil in the final
chapter. The devil manages to extract from the embar-
rassed congress of clerics the admission that the most
heinous of all crimes "are those which may be summed
up by the word 'sex'." Therefore, the devil offers Ireland immunity from such temptations, on the condi-
tion that the church would not "lay undue stress on
the wickedness of simony, nepotism, drunkenness, per-
jury and murder." When the clerics accept the bargain,
the devil then promises:

".... the clergy of this country wealth and the respect of
their people for all time. When a stranger enters a village, he will not have to ask which is the priest's house.
It will be easy of identification, for it will be the largest
house there. I promise you that whenever priests are
sought, it will not be in the houses of the poor that they
will be found. And as a sign that I will keep my part of
the bargain, I will stamp the foreheads of your priesthood
with my own particular seal—the seal of pride."

We have, then, in *The Unfortunate Fursey* a rare and
brilliant mélange of qualities: an airily imaginative jeu
d'esprit, a quaint romance, a satire that is through most
of the book so farcically broad that it disarms intol-
erance, and yet finally, behind all of these characteristics, is this stubbornly irreducible core of hard criticism. Even in Shaw, frivolity was rarely so gay and yet,
paradoxically, so seriously employed.

Sequels, so the cliché tells us, are never as good. Yet *The Return of Fursey* is nearly so, even when gauged by the high standards of the original; and when it is gauged by its own standards, which are rather different, it is very good indeed. *The Unfortunate Fursey* was a carefree spit in the eye at a malevolent and intractable world from which the main character manages, quite romantically and improbably, to escape. Yet, as we all know, no one finally escapes—not Don Quixote, not Huck Finn, not Captain Boyle, and certainly not any of those rather less complex characters known as human beings. So in *The Return of Fursey*, Wall makes amends for the escapism of the first book. Fursey is brought back to his world, Ireland, and comes to terms with it. *The Return* is, then, a basically serious book, and it might just as well have been called *The Education of the Unfortunate Fursey* or *The Coming of Age of Fursey*. Many of the high jinks and much of the inventiveness and the charm still remain, but the greatest charm of this book is it ultimate sadness.

The plot of the novel is rather less rambling than that of the first book. The King of Cashel sends a delegation to the court of Mercia in England, a delegation consisting of Fursey's old abbot and of his quondam rival Magnus. The abbot applies for the extradition of the notorious sorcerer Fursey, but Ethelwulf, Mercia's King, refuses the request, thinking that a captive sorcerer might be of use in the spring campaign against the kingdom of Strathclyde. However, Magnus and the abbot do succeed in persuading Maeve to return with them. The call of respectability is too much for her, and in any event she was originally impelled to run away with Fursey because she felt sorry for him.

Fursey is first overwhelmed by sadness and then by bitterness and finally by rage. He cries:

> "Damn respectability and virtue! . . . Henceforth I will serve Evil. I'll become a most depraved character. I'll turn really wicked. . . . I'm tired of being the football of destiny. I'll earn for myself a terrible reputation as an evil-working fellow. . . . people will say that my like for depravity has never been seen in the world before."

Having made this terrible decision, Fursey's next steps are quite clear. He must escape from Mercia before the king discovers his ineptitude as a sorcerer, he must kill Magnus, and he must recover Maeve. On the advice of the now sadly dessicated Albert, Fursey applies to his old acquaintance, the devil, who is himself rather battered, having emerged none too heroically from an encounter with that demon of virtue, the Gentle Anchorite. In return for two pieces of advice, Fursey sells his soul to the devil, the bargain being sealed by being written in Fursey's blood on a goatskin parchment which after considerable difficulty the devil forces him to swallow.

The devil's first advice is for Fursey to make his way back to Ireland by attaching himself to a nearby ship full of marauding Vikings. The Vikings are all "hardy fellows, in aspect wild, brutal and terrific beyond description," and their captain is called by the, to Fursey, very uncomfortable name of Sigurd the Skull Splitter. Despite his unprepossessing appearance, Fursey's ability to produce limitless goblets of ale by throwing his rope

over a tree, and also his promise to lead the Vikings to
the rich monastery of Clonmacnoise, persuade them to
accept him as an apprentice.

Although Fursey has determined to lead a life of
exemplary depravity, he has really very little talent for
it, and so he manages to alert the monks in time to prepare for the attack. Thinking himself now *persona non
grata* with both the Vikings and the clergy, Fursey
adopts the devil's second piece of advice, which is to
seek out Cuthbert and apprentice himself to the wizard
in order to learn the trade and therefore vanquish
Magnus. Cuthbert is now living in a commune of
supernatural outcasts, which includes wizards, crystal-
lomancers, scryers, conjurers, clairvoyants, mathemati-
cians, a ventriloquist and a reciter of poetry. Fursey
spends several months there, doing menial chores around
Cuthbert's cave, looking after a cow that he has found,
and not perceptibly growing in wickedness. Finally, he
persuades Cuthbert to concoct a love philtre with which
he hopes to win Maeve back. While the philtre is
settling, Cuthbert takes Fursey to a Witch's Sabbath
for his initiation. However, Albert causes such disrup-
tion among the other familiars, that Fursey is ignomin-
iously expelled. Returning to Cuthbert's cave, he finds
that his cow has drunk all of the love potion and now
falls violently in love with him.

Cuthbert, by this time, has had quite enough of
Fursey and sends him on his way, with a poisoned
needle to kill Magnus. Before Fursey leaves, he auctions
off Albert to the highest bidder, and is thus divested of
one of the trappings of sorcery. On his way, he manages

to divest himself of sorcery itself, for he meets a rustic
prophet so assured of his own saintliness that he allows
Fursey to breathe the wizardly spirit down his throat.
Also on the road, Fursey encounters the Devil who
wishes to claim his soul; however, Fursey points out in
a fit of seasickness on board the Viking ship he vomited
up the goatskin parchment, and in any event the parchment was not witnessed. And so Fursey proceeds airily
on, with his soul once again his own.

Magnus is surprisingly happy to see Fursey, for he
has become bored with married life and yearns to be
off to an amusing war. He even leaves Fursey alone
with Maeve for several days, rather hoping that Fursey
will waft her away once more. Maeve unfortunately
seems quite immune to Fursey's charms, and when
Magnus returns with Fursey's old abbot he finds both
still there. The monks of Clonmacnoise have now become convinced that Fursey saved them from the Vikings, and so the abbot offers to take Fursey back into the
kitchen at his old job of paring edible roots and with
the distinct possibility of promotion to the post of Lay
Brother in Charge of Poultry. At one time, such a life
was all that Fursey desired, but now he replies, "I've
changed. I've seen the world, and bitter and cruel as
it is, I belong there now. I cannot go back to the
cloister."

He cannot bring himself to kill Magnus either, but
the two dissatisfied men concoct a plot by which Magnus will go off to war and then send back news of his
presumed death, thus leaving the way open for Fursey
to win back Maeve. This plot is foiled when Maeve

announces that she is going to have Magnus's child, and so wearily Magnus puts his sword and spear and shield and corslet behind the door to gather dust. There is, then, nothing for Fursey to do but leave. Maeve does not even look up to say goodbye. The conclusion is so well written and so quietly moving that it deserves to be quoted:

> It was dusk. He did not pause, but began to plod slowly along the road which led over the hills into the unknown lands in the south. In the dim light, against the mighty backcloth of creation, the tumbled mountains and valleys over which the shadows of approaching night were gathering, he seemed a negligible figure. He was indeed a negligible figure, a small, bowed man holding his torn coat tightly about him, not only for warmth, but as if to keep from the vulgar gaze his terrors and the remnants of his dreams. And so, as he goes down the road, he is lost to view in the gathering shadows, glimpsed only for a moment at the turn of the track or against the vast night sky, just as we have managed to catch a glimpse of him through the twilight of the succeeding centuries.
>
> Last spring I walked the road from Clonmacnoise to Cashel, and from Cashel to The Gap. Fursey and the others are still there, trampled into the earth of road and field these thousand years.

In *The Return of Fursey*, Wall has done something quite remarkable. Although setting his characters in a milieu that might have been drawn by a macabre Walt Disney, he has quite transcended the limitations of the fantastic cartoon. In the first volume, Fursey was simply a vastly appealing caricature, a sweet and downtrodden buffoon; here, he acquires the dimensions of humanity. At the opening of *The Return*, Fursey is vaguely dissatisfied with his state, even though he has security, comfort, and the woman he loves. When he is deprived of Maeve, he really takes the first step toward the loss of innocence; he understands that happiness is simply the absence of unhappiness. And by the end of the book, he is rather like a George Fitzmaurice character, for the events of the story have shown him that one does not get what one wants, that one does not retreat from the world, and that one goes on. This seems to me a reflection that Wall manages to raise to some profundity, and from the farce, the fantasy, and the satire he incongruously distills poignance.

Tom Kilroy, in the only critical article of any length on Wall's work, feels that in *The Return* "there is little of the original inspiration." It seems to me, however, that despite the growing seriousness of intention, the elements of fantasy and satire are quite as plentiful and as rich as they were in the first book. The details, for instance, of the sorcerer's hooley in Chapter VI or of the Witch's Sabbath in Chapter VII are fresh, imaginative, and copious. The touches of satire throughout the book are equally pointed, and not really repetitive of much in the first book. The clerical censor investigating the library of Clonmacnoise is a broadly drawn but devastating *reductio ad absurdum* of censorship in Ireland in the 1940s. The following interchange in Chapter II about Maeve, however, may stand as an effective brief illustration of the accuracy of Wall's aim:

> The Devil shrugged his shoulders.
> "May I ask a question?"
> "Certainly," replied Fursey.
> "Was your union consummated?"

"Certainly not," said Fursey indignantly. "We both had a good Irish Catholic upbringing, and we don't know how."

Perhaps it may be argued that *The Unfortunate Fursey* was too broad in its details and too finally irresponsible in its theme to qualify as anything more reputable than an eminently engaging entertainment with a multitude of passing satiric touches. I think that *The Return* needs no such qualifications or apologies whatsoever, for it is art.

# IV

*Leaves for the Burning* was a quite successful novel which went into two editions and is being republished this year by the Irish University Press. It won a Danish competition for the best European novel of 1952, and has been translated into Danish and published in Copenhagen. John Broderick, the author of several powerful novels about Irish provincial life such as *The Waking of Willy Ryan,* has even described it as "the best Irish novel ever written." Maurice Kennedy, in a review in *Irish Writing,* No. 34, thought it "a hilarious and disturbing book, which skated delicately along the border between sordid truth and satirical extravagance, with almost complete success." However, as Graham Greene's "entertainments" are not, to my mind, finally entertaining, so neither is the "satire" in *Leaves for the Burning* finally satiric. Indeed, Mr. Wall has remarked to me that his intention in the book was to give an exact picture of Ireland as it was in the year 1952.

None of the specific details in *Leaves for the Burning* is in itself exaggerated or even improbable, but only certain kinds of details have been chosen. When detail after detail illustrates only the sordid, the mean, the base, the ugly and the petty, a superficial view might conclude that here is an extravagant, if morose, catalogue of Ireland's postwar ills. Actually, none of the details seems to me by itself viewed through the magnifying lens of the satirist. Much in the book is horrible or ghastly, but there is really nothing grotesque or exaggerated. *Leaves* is basically a realistic, albeit quite one-sided, novel. Had it not been written by the author of *The Unfortunate Fursey,* or had it been written by an early John McGahern, I wonder if it would have been regarded as satiric at all. As an indication of the selective one-sidedness of the novel, one might note that the most connotative adjectives in its very first paragraph are these:

uneasy, dull, dark, undigested, fitful, aching, clammy, defensive, disagreeable, horrid, dreadful.

And easily the most arresting nouns in the paragraph are these:

torpor, dark, stomach, heat, shadows, effort, nightmare.

The tone of these words sets the tone and indicates the selective rationale of the whole novel, and so most assuredly anyone who comes to *Leaves for the Burning* expecting another jolly romp like *The Unfortunate Fursey* will be vastly disappointed. Sean O'Faolain called this novel in *The Listener* a "half-bitter book." It is, to my mind, considerably more than half-bitter.

What Wall is saying by the grim and depressing incidents of the novel is that this is Ireland in the 1940s

and the early 1950s. This is its spirit, its essence. And
his conclusion from the welter of evidence is that it is
a benighted country, ruled by Philistinism and jobbery
and evoking only an impoverishment of the human
spirit. This was the same conclusion that O'Casey also
drew and that he depicted in his late plays. In earlier
years, it was the conclusion that Brinsley MacNamara
had drawn in novels like *The Valley of the Squinting
Windows,* or that some years later Liam O'Flaherty had
drawn in *Mr. Gilhooley,* or that in our own time John
McGahern has drawn in *The Barracks.* Wall is not so
mournful as O'Casey or so irascible as MacNamara, or
so depressed as McGahern, but he partakes of something of all of those qualities. In the landscape of his Ireland, the worst are full of passionate intensity and the
best lack all conviction; and yet who is to say that his
case is overstated? These were the darkest days of the
book censorship, the days of the ignominious hassle over
O'Connor's translation of *The Midnight Court,* of the
persecution of the Tailor and Anstey, of Maria Duce,
of Gaelic pantomimes at the Abbey Theatre—one could
go on interminably.

The plot of *Leaves* depicts a messy, casual sprawl of
events. Wall admittedly does not plan his novels out
in advance. When writing one chapter, he often does
not know what the next will be about. His meticulous
revisions do not restucture the incidents of the plot,
but patch up the faults of the style. Here, however, the
incidents do coalesce to prove the theme, and the rambling, ambling, drunken journey of Wall's quartet of
anti-heroes does appropriately objectify the aimlessness

of their lives. Broadly, the novel is structured like this: in the first hundred pages Wall gives a leisurely exposition of the dreary, humdrum life in an Irish village, and this section culminates in an inadvertent, communal murder that occurs during an after-hours drinking bout. In the second hundred pages, Wall shows how four middle-aged men who were in the shebeen flee in panic to Dublin, and then decide to make a pilgrimage to Sligo where Yeats's remains are about to be re-interred in Drumcliffe Churchyard. This journey becomes a prolonged drinking bout, and none of them reaches Sligo. One by one, they drop out to return to their pasts, and the section concludes with the main character, Lucian Brewse Burke, proposing to and being rejected by the woman he once loved and could have married. The point of the section seems to be that nothing can be salvaged from the shambles of the past, and Lucian returns to the fantastically dreary job of a very minor County Council official in an appallingly ugly and thoroughly Philistine country village.

Had the novel ended here, it would have been an inordinately depressing catalogue of personal defeat and social debasement. However, there is a short coda of twenty pages in which Lucian makes a brave, ineffectual, and quixotic attempt to defend his office from robbery. He is wounded and hospitalized, and, although his action was in itself absurd, it is very nearly the saving of the novel. When Lucian, the feckless, middle-aged futility rises to the defense of the one and eightpence of government money, he has managed a small triumph of the spirit. It is a triumph that predictably

is not recognized by what we call today the power structure, but it is recognized by the red-haired man who
shot him, and who gives him later a gift of a pack of
cigarettes. That is all Lucian will or could get in this
milieu, but it is perhaps enough to establish the value
of the human spirit. As Lucian's friend Frank wrote
him:

> I do not know the details of your adventure so that I am
> unable to judge of its foolishness or its grandeur. I only
> know that for the past hour since reading of it I have
> been laughing, and at the same time been very near to
> tears. I had always thought you a singularly futile per-
> son; but now with the newspaper headline staring me
> in the face, I no longer know. Perhaps you and I and
> our kind are not so ineffective as I have thought. Per-
> haps our pride and the tradition in which we were
> brought up, the houses which taught us little but at
> least never taught us a pliant knee, have given us some-
> thing which we can contribute to the life of today, so
> that another voice may continue to be heard alongside
> the cry of the huckster which sounds from every corner
> of the land.

Or, as the red-haired man said more succinctly:

> . . . breeding's a queer thing. It always comes out. It's
> all the same in dogs or horses or in men. It can turn an
> unlikely man into something like a hero just for the
> moment, because there's an instinctive pride in him.

Lucian's triumph does not affect in any significant
way the waste of ugliness, spiritual impoverishment,
and ignominious motives that make up Wall's picture
of Ireland. And probably it is not enough of a triumph
to overcome the meticulously built up aura of depres-

sion that arises from most of the details of the book. If, however, one is prepared to settle for what reasonable assertions the human spirit may make in an uncongenial universe, if one does not demand the Scarlet Pimpernelish triumphs of Fursey knocking down Magnus and swooping off with Maeve, then it must probably be admitted that Wall has plausibly stated a realistic case.

This is hardly a book that evokes affection, but much in it does certainly compel admiration. It is, for the most part, the admiration that arises from the recognition of the truth of the details, rather than from the pleasure about how a detail has been cunningly heightened or exaggerated in order to exhibit what is wrong with it. For instance:

> Lucian's place of work was a single room which the County Council rented from the owner of a bicycle repair shop. A signboard which read "County of Moynell: County Council Sub-Office" had many years previously fallen from its place over the door of the shop and had remained ever since on the pavement propped against the wall beneath the window. To get to the sub-office you entered the bicycle shop, stepping carefully in the half-dark between the piled bits of long-dead bicycles and around the up-ended ones undergoing repair, until you came to a door at the far end of the shop. This opened directly into the County Council sub-office, which was a single room divided in two by a counter. It was an annex to the original building, a sort of shed with a corrugated iron roof, and walls stained by long fingers of damp. Indeed, so damp was the interior that official forms, if left too long in the one place on the shelves, became quite unusable. Bundles of forms with gummed backs acquired the consistency of a wooden block, which, Lucian and his assistant had found, made an excellent

fuel. There was no sanitary accommodation; and when
it rained, the rain came through the roof in many places.
If the shower was light, it could be avoided by moving
your table from one spot to another; but in the event of
a downpour the only thing to do was to vacate the office
altogether and stand in the doorway of the bicycle shop
where you would still be available to anyone calling on
County Council business. The rafters supporting the
corrugated iron roof were gossamered by the webs of
many spiders, and they and various other hardy races of
insects lived, reproduced their kind and died in that
shadowy world high above the electric light shades. The
more foolhardy or careless fell from time to time into
the office below, which frightened them very much indeed, to judge by the wild scamper they made for safety
across tables, forms and papers. The chief disadvantage
of the office, however, was a far door opening into a
yard in which the landlord kept a pig and some ema-
ciated poultry. The bicycleman, his wife and five children, his brother-in-law and a dog all considered that
they had a right-of-way, so that there was a constant
coming and going all day long. Each year for ten years
on the first day of January Lucian had addressed a
minute to his headquarters in Moymell, the county
town, calling attention to the state of the premises. A
reply came invariably to hand sometime in February to
the effect that the matter was being accorded attention.

This appalling office is built up of exactly observed,
realistic details, rather than by the quick swoop and
pounce of the satirist who turns his magnifying glass
upon one or two absurdities, and thus proves the grotes-
query of the whole. There are, here and there, in the
novel heightened and not always successful touches of
satire; at one point Lucian stops in front of the local
corrugated iron cinema to observe next week's attrac-
tion and finds it to be "Peerless Paula Punk in 'The

Marvellous Magdalene.' " O'Duffy could have written this, and it might not have been out of place in Wall's next novel, *No Trophies Raise*. Here, however, it is simply out of tone with the surrounding mass of realistic detail.

The realism is equally effective in the mass of details which Wall uses to build up his principal characters. Lucian as the protagonist is, of course, the most fully developed, and he is no Fursey, no caricature. We know his past, his childhood, his feelings toward his parents, his ambitions, dissatisfactions, his relations with his superiors, with his inferiors, with his friends. He exists realistically and fully. If he is not going to have any notably prominent existence in any reader's memory, nevertheless a reader regards him with an interesting mixture of feelings—with sympathy, with irritation, with occasional contempt, and even with occasional admiration. He is unarguably a realistic and not a satiric character.

The incidents of the novel are similarly effective because one recognizes the truth of the specific details. The drinking scenes seem to me absolutely just, and the way in which Wall contrives to have a multitude of details fuzz up, then briefly merge into sharp clarity, and then hazily dissolve is brilliantly persuasive. To choose one paragraph from a long and closely knit passage is impossible; however:

Lucian's wandering gaze suddenly encountered his own reflection in the corner of a framed glass advertisement for Guinness' Stout which hung on the opposite wall. He saw that his irongrey hair was slightly tossed, and that his face was puffed and flushed. His horn-rimmed glasses were a little askew, and from behind them two dulled eyes stared back at him from a stupid and silly-looking face. "I'm drunk," he muttered, "very, very, very drunk."

The realist is much more constrained by his material than is the satirist. Both aim, of course, at truth, but the satirist may pervert the specific truth of individual details in order to arrive at whatever spiritual truth he has in mind. The realist's approach is more phlegmatic, and he arrives at truth by a selection and arrangement of the recognizable. Or to oversimplify, one might say that the satirist draws cartoons and the realist arranges photographs. Some of Wall's photographs are most meaningfully chosen; for instance, there is considerable point to be derived from the fact that his four anti-heroes in the central portion of the book are going to the funeral of Yeats. More than any one man, Yeats can be seen as an emblem of the best of Irish aspirations—as, indeed, the conscience of his race. It is hardly over-reading the book to note the disparity between Yeats and Wall's heroes, or to note that Yeats is dead, or to derive some meaning from Wall's quartet never finally arriving at the funeral.

*Leaves for the Burning* is not written from quite so narrow a vantage point as *The Valley of the Squinting Windows* or *The Barracks,* but its ending is not significant enough or strong enough to counteract the prevailingly bleak tone. There are, of course, many excellent works that survey the same ground as Wall's in this novel, and survey it in a single tone—a novel or two by Honor Tracy, a novel by Anthony Cronin, some of the late plays of O'Casey even, many others—and I suspect that my own preference is simply a preference for light-heartedness over glumness. Perhaps I am fumbling toward a definition of the pseudo work of art, although I do not like the pejorative overtones of "pseudo." Such a work, however, may contain artifice, craftsmanship, brilliance, any quality that one may find in a work of art. But unless it also views life fully, in a variety of tones, from a number of vantage points, it is simply a melodrama or a farce masquerading as a tragedy or a comedy. About 200 of the 217 pages of *Leaves for the Burning* seem to me such a masquerade. From the standpoint of my own biases, the best that I can say is that these 200 pages are an admirably wrought masquerade.

# V

Wall's last published novel, *No Trophies Raise,* also surveys the contemporary Irish scene, but in a less realistic and much less personal fashion than did *Leaves for the Burning.* The Lucian Brewse Burke of *Leaves* was, I think, something of a painful self-portrait, and the sullen anger of the book was the long pent-up reaction of a much-bruised psyche. *No Trophies* is not a thoroughly satisfying novel, but it is a much more "created" one than was *Leaves for the Burning. Leaves* strikes me finally as very talented and selective observation; *No Trophies* observes and then heightens what it selects. Satire, a minor tool in *Leaves,* is perhaps the chief auctorial strategy in *No Trophies Raise,* and certain reviewers even thought that the satire was a bit overdone. An anonymous reviewer in *The Dublin Magazine* defended Wall from the charge, remarking, "those English critics who have protested that the fantasy is too extravagant might profitably examine the correspondence columns of Irish newspapers, and the reports of borough and town council meetings." In Ireland, perhaps more than in most places, life tends to defeat satire by outdoing it; that poses a problem for the satirist, but it is hardly his fault.

Wall's intention in this novel seems to be a comic indictment of much of the public and private morality of post-war Ireland. This was a period which in 1956, when the novel was published, had not been much written of, and which was in certain respects different from the Ireland of the 1930s and 1940s. Mainly, the new Ireland was becoming much less insular; it was an Ireland which would shortly be applying for membership in the European Economic Community, which would be taking a notable part in the debates and activities of the United Nations, and which would be, above all, striving to join the modern world by the conventional manner of making more money, by raising and, therefore, considerably altering the nature of its standard of living and the tastes and desires of its citizens. Consequently, the cast of characters in Wall's novel is rather large, and there are two principal plot strands which are not closely intertwined until the closing chapters.

Briefly, the two plots work like this: first, "Pig Feed" Sam Welply, a brilliant embodiment of venality and rural business cunning, is branching out from his successful pig feed business into the new opportunities offered by the tourist trade. He has built a luxury hotel by the Lake of Killarney, and he proposes to the Minister for Arts and Crafts that the hotel be opened by an international convention or congress. He does not at all care what kind of convention—just so it has publicity value. Here, the other strand of the plot is picked up.

The Minister of Arts and Crafts, a smoothly drawn picture of urbanity and practicality, has given a lecture on the philosophy of Albert Thomas Hand, whose work he has read in the German-Swiss publication *Der Philosoph,* and whom he declares uncategorically to be "probably the greatest philosopher the world has produced in the last hundred years." He also remarks, "Now, there's a man fortunate enough to be doing the work for which nature fitted him, and doing it supremely well." In fact, Albert Thomas Hand is no German philosopher, but an aging, grossly underpaid, and quite ignored minor Civil Servant in the minister's own department. The minister arranges, then, that Pig-Feed Sam's hotel be opened by an international philosophical congress which shall feature the reading of a paper by Hand. This unexpected fame does not, however, help the aging Hand to get a long overdue promotion; indeed, he is once again passed over, and faces the prospect of retiring shortly on a small and inadequate pension. Further, his speech at the convention is far from a success. He also catches pneumonia, takes to his bed, dies, and, as he has no money, is buried in a pauper's grave. His death would, of course, be unfortunate publicity for the tourist trade, and so Pig Feed Sam has it efficiently hushed up. He says:

"You didn't seriously think that I was going to buy a grave for him? The funeral and burial will be chargeable to public funds of course. Now, the Minister told me that Hand hadn't a relative in the world, so there's no one need be informed. That's a blessing. Before you visit the office of the local authority, ask the doctor who attended the old man, for a death certificate and bring it with you. . . . I want you also to be present this evening when the old man is coffined. . . . When it's done, see that the coffin is taken discreetly off the premises by the back door."

This is an appropriately ghastly conclusion to sum up Wall's feelings about the relations of culture and business in contemporary Ireland. His two main strands of plot have a multitude of coldly cutting details, and alone they would have combined to fashion a hard Jonsonian-Molièrian satiric comedy.

This toughness, however, is softened by a sub-plot of considerable length, involving Pig-Feed Sam's son Eugene. Eugene is a well-meaning, but not particularly remarkable or interesting young man, and his story shows how Pig-Feed Sam inexorably bends Eugene to his will—to give up one girl, to propose to another, and to prepare himself to be an effective business man. The sub-plot allows Wall to introduce certain satiric topics, such as jobbery and the Knights of Columbanus, and it allows him to introduce us to the morality of business as the neophyte Eugene learns it through the tutelage of his buccaneer of a father. Satire, however, is not the main intention of this sub-plot. Eugene is a type, but a realistic type. He has enough good will and perception to deplore his father's tactics, but is finally too weak to resist the attractions of money and security. Through him, Wall is able to dramatize the conflict of values in Ireland, and to show how venality triumphs.

There are, to my mind, two objections to the sub-plot. First, it is soft rather than satiric in tone. Eugene feels the poignance of Hand's death, and his feelings are meant undoubtedly to help evoke our own. There is some disparity, then, between the effects evoked by the main plot and by the sub-plot. One asks us to react intellectually to certain immoral grotesqueries; the other asks us to react emotionally to their effects. On the one hand, we are asked to note that this civilization is absurd and abominable; on the other, we are asked to feel that it is not only abominable but also sad. Sentiment and satire can, of course, co-exist, but their wedding, as in the Fursey books, is something of a tour de force. In *No Trophies Raise,* the sentiment seems to dilute the satire. Perhaps the difference between the success of this union in the Fursey books and its failure here is that here the soft sub-plot is simply an overt restatement of what the main plots have sufficiently said, while in the Fursey books the softness was an integral part of the statement. I am not particularly happy with this explanation, and, indeed, I am not quite sure that it even makes sense.

A second objection to the sub-plot is that it takes up so much space. Eugene is not the character that Pig-Feed Sam is or that Hand could be, and one wants to see a good deal more of them than one does. Indeed, the Hand plot seems even in a couple of instances scanted, and lacks what practitioners of the well-made play would years ago have called the obligatory scene. One wants to see the first meeting of Hand with the Minister after the Minister has learned who the old man is, and also one wants to see a part of Hand's address to the convention.

Some reviewers have objected to the plot in toto.

Maurice Kennedy thought that Wall did not "seem to be quite certain of what exactly he is satirizing," and that "The various themes of the story are laid down and taken up with mechanical regularity, and little inevitability, and tied roughly and improbably together at the end. . . ." Tom Kilroy agreed emphatically:

> In fact Mr. Wall is never quite sure whom he is writing about, as the chief character in the book seems to be Sam's spineless, helpless son Eugene, who appears and re-appears at intervals in a series of meaningless, negative incidents. The final chapter closes with the death of the philosopher, unwanted and unappreciated by his countrymen, an ending which is repulsive in its sentimentality and in its obvious, laboured conclusion.
>
> It is surprising, then, that there is distinguished writing and intelligent social satire in such a bad short novel. . . .

The problem of the plot, I think, is not its arrangement and certainly not any confusion in the author's mind about what his subject was. The incidents of the various plot strands all contribute to his theme, and their illustrative juxtaposition is probably the most conventional and time-honored structure that one could ask for in a comic novel of any scope.

Predictably, the novel has an abundance of passing excellences of the kind which I have illustrated in the discussions of the earlier books. Although dozens of drolly pointed individual touches are not enough, without some strong help from the plot, to impose a fully satisfying unity, they are certainly enough to keep one reading pleasurably on.

# VI

Wall's prose style deserves a word. It has sometimes been said to exemplify Irish gigantism, a piling up of words for their own sake and for the author's delight in them, as one often finds in Joyce, Beckett, Flann O'Brien, and Eimar O'Duffy. Wall's playfulness with words is a strong symptom of his sense of fun, but for the most part his style does not seem to me nearly so flamboyant or highly colored as O'Brien's or O'Duffy's. It is generally an unobtrusive plain style that is very good of its kind. Comic effects can be obtained by any number of rhetorical devices, but in the long run it seems to me that these devices must be firmly anchored to a basically plain style like Wall's. Rhetorical devices are, in one sense, excesses of style, and so to be effective their excess needs a norm to be measured against. "Proper words in proper places," said Dean Swift, and certainly *in petto* the argument may be illustrated by considering the stylistic necessities of any effective joke, which requires, above all, simplicity, order, and exactness.

Often, Wall's style appears rather bare of rhetorical

devices. Some comic writers, such as O'Casey, seem to achieve a large proportion of their effects by their form rather than by their content. Wall, I think, relies much more upon a comic content which he then relates by a simple, tight, generally unadorned style. As a writer of comedy, his strength is as much in his perception as in his execution. The execution is not, of course, lame or ineffective; a tight Swiftian clarity is perhaps the most exacting of styles.

The greatest deviation from this style comes in the Fursey novels which are related, both in the narrative and in the dialogue, with a mildly formal diction that is often in droll contrast with a distinctly informal action. Here, for instance, is Wall's description of a night Fursey spent in the cell of The Gentle Anchorite:

> Before long the cave was shrill with the hermit's catarrhal snores which forced their way through his beard in a muffled whistle.
> Hour after hour Fursey tossed on the straw unable to sleep. When a man of determined sanctity has lived in a small cave for forty years, the insect life is apt to assume alarming proportions. Bugs, resigned for many years to the thin diet which the hermit's skinny frame provided, after one nip at Fursey scuttled off to tell their friends, and soon all the game in the cavern were making in his direction. They came in such myriads that for a moment Fursey thought that an attempt was being made to murder him. Plump fleas investigated different parts of his body in a series of gargantuan hops, while great strapping bugs fastened themselves to his arms and thighs. The smaller fry of the insect world, mites and the like, contented themselves with setting up colonies in unlikely corners of his anatomy where the competition was less keen. Fursey rolled and wallowed, but to no avail. To add to his discomfort The Gentle Anchorite woke up

and seemed not only jealous of the attention his vermin were paying to Fursey, but to fear that there was a real danger of losing the external evidence of his forty years' sanctity, so he bent over from time to time to collect as many bugs as he could from Fursey's body and put them back on his own. This preposterous behaviour Fursey found in the highest degree exasperating. In his opinion it only encouraged the most mischievous of the bugs to greater liveliness, and it obviated all possibility of sleep. You couldn't possibly sleep if you were turned over every half-an-hour by your host and searched.

This seems to me a basically plain style, in which most of the words are defensible either for their syntax or their sense. There are a few places where a word might be pared away, but the passage is generally quite tightly written. A plain style is usually not only straightforward in syntax, as is this passage, but it also is straightforward and simple in diction. In a few instances, in phrases such as "apt to assume alarming proportions" or "the external evidence of his forty years' sanctity" or "in the highest degree exasperating," Wall deviates for purpose of comic incongruity into the mildly formal, and usually when he does he achieves his effect. Only rarely does he seem to nod; for instance, the phrase "in the highest degree" appears frequently in the Fursey books.

On those occasions when he needs it, Wall can also gain considerable effect purely by sentence structure. Much of the moving effect of the final paragraphs of both of the Fursey books, which I have already quoted, derives from the arrangement of the sentences. In the conclusion of *The Return,* he seems to attain his effect largely by his placement of prepositional phrases. The prepositional phrase is not generally considered, except in rather formal parallelisms, to be a strong device. Nevertheless, much of the mournfulness in the conclusion derives, I think, from his placement of these phrases. Consider, for instance, sentences like:

> He did not pause, but began to plod slowly along the road which led over the hills into the unknown lands in the south. In the dim light, against the mighty backcloth of creation, the tumbled mountains and valleys over which the shadows of approaching night were gathering, he seemed a negligible figure.

Here, the strongest part of the sentences, the part contributing most to the mournful effect, seems to be the cunningly used series of phrases.

One of Wall's most appealing characteristics is that he writes with charm, sympathy and understanding of life's underdogs. If one were to draw a composite Wall hero, he would be a middle-aged man with failing powers, an incipient paunch, and a poor paying job of dull drudgery. A man with no presence, no "charisma," shy, ineffectual, inevitably passed over, one of the gentle, unassuming, and unsuccessful people who mutely lead lives of quiet desperation.

And yet he would also be a man of sensitivity, reading, taste, and a basic good will. Even as his life is frittered away, he yet would retain a small, intractably stubborn core to him, and he would occasionally wrest a small, socially unimportant, perhaps only symbolical triumph from the recalcitrant, disinterested, and possibly malignant universe he inhabits.

This occasional victory has been the cause probably of the charge of sentimentality which has sometimes been leveled at Wall. Superficially, it would seem that a sentimental satirist is a contradiction in terms. It is certainly true that the great satirists have written works that were unremittingly hard in their castigation of folly, but I am not at all certain that a touch of sentiment is a fault in satire, or even that the rare writer may not seek to evoke a hard, satiric and a soft, sentimental reaction simultaneously. This is a rare effect, indeed, but it is also a magnificent one. I can think of a number of such instances: the droll, sad, ineffable conclusion of Chaplin's *City Lights;* the poignant and absurd moment in Chekhov's *The Cherry Orchard* when Varya is sent in to receive Lopahin's proposal of marriage and manages to muff it; the exquisite and adolescent love of Romeo and Juliet in the balcony scene, which delights us by its lyricism at the same time that it charms us by its naivete. I do not think that Wall quite attains this fusion in *No Trophies Raise,* but he does approach it in *Leaves for the Burning,* and, to my mind, he beautifully reaches it in *The Return of Fursey.*

A similar criticism probably attaches to whimsy. *The Virginia Kirkus Bulletin,* an American periodical which attempts, I suppose, to measure the middlebrow commercial attractiveness of new books, remarked of *The Unfortunate Fursey* that "this has little of general appeal to the American market." Behind that view lies the attitude that whimsy is simply satire without point. By extension, then, a fantasy is simply a group of co-hering whimsies padded out to a certain length. I hardly think that pure fantasy needs defense. Shakespeare's Forest of Arden and Carroll's Wonderland are simply too delightful to require any pedestrian critical buttressing. However, if a defense were to be made, it might well begin by noting that a successful, individual, memorable fantasy is a rare and remarkable symptom of the human imagination and, therefore, I should suppose, of one of the essential qualities of humanity itself.

Wall's Fursey books are not, of course, pure fantasies but satiric fantasies in which the pointed coexists with the simply playful. I would think this a healthy union, for it prevents an excess of morality from tilting the satire away from the comic to the intensely moral, such as perhaps we get in the final, too moral, or even immoral book of *Gulliver's Travels*. Fantasy demands creation, fancy, artifice, and is therefore a lightening, humanizing force, a humane balance, and a guard against fanaticism.

The work of Mervyn Wall illustrates this point. When he was most overtly concerned with condemning the follies of his time and country in the novel *Leaves for the Burning,* he was bleakly convincing. With the greater emotional distance of *No Trophies Raise,* he became somewhat more engagingly convincing. When he combined that emotional distance with the intellectual distance of fantasy in *The Unfortunate Fursey,* he was both convincing and delightful. And finally, when he was able to weld sympathy in an integral fashion to these other qualities, as he did in *The Return of Fursey,* he made us accept even bleakness with a sprightly and philosophic heart.

# Bibliography

I. *Principal Works*

"They Also Serve," *Harper's Magazine*, 181 (July 1940), 125–129.

*Alarm among the Clerks*. Dublin: The Richview Press, 1940.

"Adventure," *Capuchin Annual* (Dublin, 1943), 65–71.

"The Hogskin Gloves," *Capuchin Annual* (Dublin, 1944).

"The Demon Angler," *Capuchin Annual* (Dublin, 1945–1946), 53–58.

*The Unfortunate Fursey*. London: The Pilot Press, 1946; New York: Crown Publishers, 1947; Dublin: The Helicon Press, 1965.

"Metamorphosis of a Licensed Vintner," *Capuchin Annual* (Dublin, 1947); also published under the title of "Hair on a Billiard Ball," *Collier's*, 119 (January 11, 1947), 29.

"Cloonaturk," *Argosy* (London), VIII (December 1947), 89–98.

*The Return of Fursey*. London: The Pilot Press, 1948.

"Leo the Terror," *Collier's*, 122 (November 27, 1948), 14–15; also published under the title of "Leo the

Lion," *Irish Writing,* 7 (February 1949) , 7–22.

"Age Cannot Wither," *The Irish Red Cross Annual* (1951), 52–56.

*Leaves for the Burning.* London: Methuen, 1952; New York: Devin Adair, 1952; and under the Danish title of *Den Helt Store Tur,* Copenhagen: Ascheboug Dansk Forlag, 1953.

"Extract from an Abandoned Novel," *Irish Writing,* 29 (December 1954) , 17–28.

*No Trophies Raise.* London: Methuen, 1956.

*Forty Foot Gentlemen Only.* Dublin: Allen Figgis, 1962.

"The Men Who Could Outstare Cobras," *Capuchin Annual* (Dublin, 1966) , 74–80.

*The Lady in the Twilight.* Newark, Delaware: Proscenium Press, 1971.

There are also many ephemeral reviews in Irish periodicals, such as the *Irish Times,* the *Evening Press, Irish Writing* and *The Bell.* A good deal of unpublished material exists, including an abandoned novel, a children's satire, a play, and many radio scripts. Some of Wall's manuscripts are housed in the Library of the University of Texas.

II. *Works about Wall*

Very little has been written about Wall. Other than the usual superficial book reviews, there has, indeed, been only one essay written about his fiction: Thomas Kilroy, "Mervyn Wall: The Demands of Satire," *Studies,* 47 (Spring 1958) , 83–89. The only worthwhile and generally available comment on his playwriting is a theatre review by Denis Johnston in *The Bell* for 1941.